Jesus' Birth, Death, and Resurrection

Geary Reid

All Scripture quotations are from the King James Version unless otherwise noted.

ISBN: 978-976-8305-92-3.

Acknowledgments

Great thanks must be expressed to the following people:

The heavenly Father, for granting me the wisdom and inspiration to record the information in this book, which I began on April 25, 2022, and completed on April 28, 2022; my family, for their continued encouragement and support regarding various challenges; and several people who have assisted with reviewing and editing the book:

- Pastor Jocelyn Dolphin
- Rev. Rickford Fanfair
- Rendell F. Harry

To you, the reader: have fun while reading, and grasp and practice what you learn so that this world will become a better place. Many people are depending on your guidance. We all need a shoulder to lean on and a hand to guide us.

Rev. Geary Reid

MBA, FCCA, FAAPM, MPM, CAT

Reid's Learning Institute and Business Consultancy

reidnlearn.com

Amazon: amazon.com/author/gearyreid

Facebook: Reid n Learn

Instagram: Reid n Learn

LinkedIn: Reid's Learning Institute
and Business Consultancy

199 Kuru - Kururu, Soesdyke Linden Highway
Guyana, South America

Table of Contents

Introduction

Jesus came to the earth because Adam and Eve had sinned. It was the first sin, and that first sin caused them to lose their status in the garden of Eden. God was angry with their decision to eat of the tree that was in the center of the garden, so he enforced sanctions on the serpent, Eve and Adam. However, God is a merciful God who wants to save humanity, so he had to establish an immediate plan to do so. The redemptive plan to save mankind was made available through Jesus Christ.

The birth of Jesus was prophesied long before he visited the earth. Persons need to know that Jesus existed before Adam and Eve. Indeed, he was involved in the creation of the world. Therefore, he was aware of the first sin from the beginning.

When Jesus came to the earth, he came for sinners. He avoided the religious people and often associated with those who needed salvation. He is a Savior for everyone. He wanted to save people from their sins and to give them a new beginning. Since humans were separated from God because of their sins, Jesus came to reconcile man unto God.

Jesus' purpose was revealed many centuries ago. Therefore, when Jesus came, he walked in the purpose that was assigned for him.

Mary and Joseph are often referred to as Jesus' parents. However, God performed a miracle that caused Mary to become pregnant before she and Joseph knew each other. While Joseph wanted to put away Mary because she was pregnant, God worked through the angels to convince him to accept her. Joseph was placed into a deep sleep, and the angel told him important things. King Herod thought he could prevent the birth of Jesus, but all of his plans failed, because God protected his Son Jesus, along with Mary and Joseph. Jesus' birth and assignment could not be stopped by King Herod.

The death of Jesus was predicted in advance. He even informed his disciples about it three times. He was not afraid to tell them about his death and how it would happen. Jesus had all the details about his death, and he shared the sequence of events with his disciples. Before Judas betrayed Jesus, Jesus already knew that it would happen. The events leading up to Jesus' death were fulfilled according to the sequence he foretold to his disciples.

Jesus' crucifixion was painful, but necessary, as he had to die for the sins of humanity. When the people requested that Barabbas be released instead of Jesus, it allowed the plan of God to be fulfilled. When Jesus was placed in the tomb, the religious leaders thought it was the end of him. They also placed guards to protect his tomb and to prevent him from arising after the third day. However, no tomb could hold Jesus back, so he arose from the tomb and visited many persons. Today, he lives in the hearts of those who accept him as Lord and Savior.

1. Adam and Eve's actions and God's responses

In the beautiful garden God created, he allowed Adam to be the first tenant and gardener. Adam was to operate as an agent for the principal. He had great authority in the garden, with one minor restriction, and that was not to "eat of the tree of the knowledge of good and evil" (Genesis 2:17).

Adam did not have to pay rent for his occupancy in the garden. His supply of food was readily available to him without having to pay for it (Genesis 2:16). Most persons would be satisfied to live in a house they did not build and accept most of the facilities in the house.

1.1 Direct access to the principal

Sometimes, persons rent properties but do not know, nor have ever seen, the principal. However, with Adam and Eve, they knew the principal and had direct access to him. The principal for the garden was the almighty God, who sees and knows everything.

1.2 Adam's responsibility and restriction in the garden

When God placed Adam in the garden, he gave him responsibilities. This was not a vacation for Adam. From the beginning when God placed Adam in the garden, Adam knew his restrictions. The tenancy agreement between God and Adam was communicated, so Adam knew what he was expected to do and what his restrictions were.

Genesis 2:8-17

⁸ And the LORD God planted a garden eastward in Eden; and there he put the man whom he had formed. ⁹ And out of the ground made the LORD God to grow every tree that is pleasant

to the sight, and good for food; the tree of life also in the midst of the garden, and the tree of knowledge of good and evil.

[10] And a river went out of Eden to water the garden; and from thence it was parted, and became into four heads. [11] The name of the first is Pison: that is it which compasseth the whole land of Havilah, where there is gold; [12] And the gold of that land is good: there is bdellium and the onyx stone. [13] And the name of the second river is Gihon: the same is it that compasseth the whole land of Ethiopia. [14] And the name of the third river is Hiddekel: that is it which goeth toward the east of Assyria. And the fourth river is Euphrates.

[15] And the LORD God took the man, and put him into the garden of Eden to dress it and to keep it. [16] And the LORD God commanded the man, saying, Of every tree of the garden thou mayest freely eat: [17] But of the tree of the knowledge of good and evil, thou shalt not eat of it: for in the day that thou eatest thereof thou shalt surely die.

If there was any misunderstanding about the tenancy agreement, then Adam could have sought God's interpretation as he continued to live in God's property. If tenants violate any of their landlord's requirements, they may face sanctions. Adam and Eve violated God's restriction, and this caused God to respond differently.

1.3 The serpent changed the line of communication

When God placed the first man in the garden, he gave him a specific assignment and communicated it to him (Genesis 2:15-17). As Eve's husband, Adam then ensured that Eve was informed of the tenancy agreement (Genesis 3:2-3). However, the serpent communicated with Eve, and then she communicated with Adam.

It is clear that Satan did not follow the same line of communication God used. Satan had his own plan, and so he spoke to Eve first, instead of talking with the man to whom God gave the assignment.

Figure 1. Lines of communication used by God and the serpent to speak to Adam and Eve

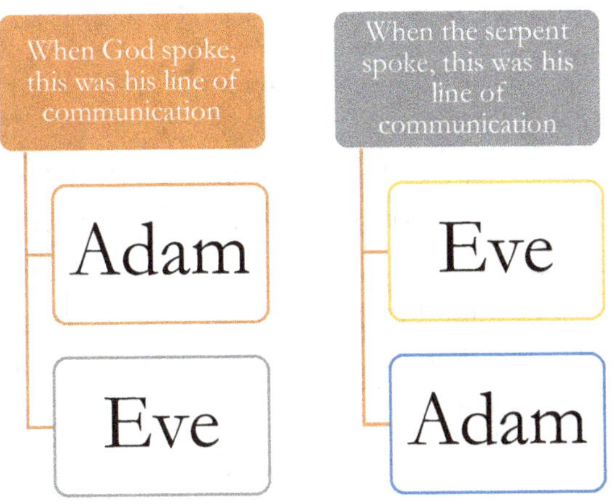

(All figures developed by the author unless otherwise noted.)

When God spoke, he communicated with Adam, but when the serpent spoke, he communicated with Eve. The serpent was and continues to be a deceiver. Adam was the first person God spoke to, and he probably had more information than Eve had. When parents will be out of the house for a short period and have to leave the children at home, they may give instructions to the eldest child about what must be done. Therefore, if anyone wants to communicate with the children in the absence of their parents, the communication should flow through the eldest child. However, the serpent started from the bottom of the chain of command.

1.4 Eve and Satan's conversation

Genesis 3:1 provides the background information that the serpent was very crafty and skillful at deception. While the serpent knows the truth, he will alter it so as to cause persons to perceive that his lies are truths.

The serpent first approached Eve (Genesis 3:1). That is a clear sign that the serpent had his deceptive plan and wanted to sell it to his potential customers. A good sales representative will approach their potential customer and have a healthy conversation. The conversation never starts in hostility, but in a friendly enough manner to cause the potential customer to be open enough to speak freely, rather than providing yes or no answers.

The first conversation from the serpent was a question. His intention in starting with a question was already a trick that he had planned. Because it was an open-ended question, Eve provided additional information in her first response. What Eve did not recognize is that she was talking with a deceiver, and he had already broken down the barriers of communication between himself and her. After the serpent got Eve to speak once, then he thought she might be more inclined to have further conversation.

Eve was guilty of giving the serpent more information than he asked for (Genesis 3:2-3), which is something that many persons get caught up in.

The serpent included God in his conversation. However, he presented a negative side of God to Eve, with the intention of letting Eve see God as her enemy. If Eve agreed that God was her enemy by preventing her from having wisdom, then she would be comfortable with turning her attention from God and listening to the serpent.

Genesis 3:1-5

[1] Now the serpent was more subtil than any beast of the field which the LORD God had made. And he said unto the woman, Yea, hath God said, Ye shall not eat of every tree of the garden? [2] And the woman said unto the serpent, We may eat of the fruit of the trees of the garden: [3] But of the fruit of the tree which is in the midst of the garden, God hath said, Ye shall not eat of it, neither shall ye touch it, lest ye die. [4] And the serpent said unto the woman, Ye shall not surely die: [5] For God doth know that in the day ye eat thereof, then your eyes shall be opened, and ye shall be as gods, knowing good and evil.

The serpent never forced Eve to eat the fruit. Because the serpent modified God's instruction to Adam, Eve felt the serpent had presented her with accurate information and was willing to go against the instruction of God. After all, her wisdom would increase and she would be like a god. If the serpent had spoken to Adam, then Adam would have either ignored him or told him of the full tenancy agreement, which also included the restriction.

Genesis 3:6

⁶And when the woman saw that the tree was good for food, and that it was pleasant to the eyes, and a tree to be desired to make one wise, she took of the fruit thereof, and did eat, and gave also unto her husband with her; and he did eat.

Figure 2. Eve's perception of the tree in the middle of the garden (Genesis 3:6)

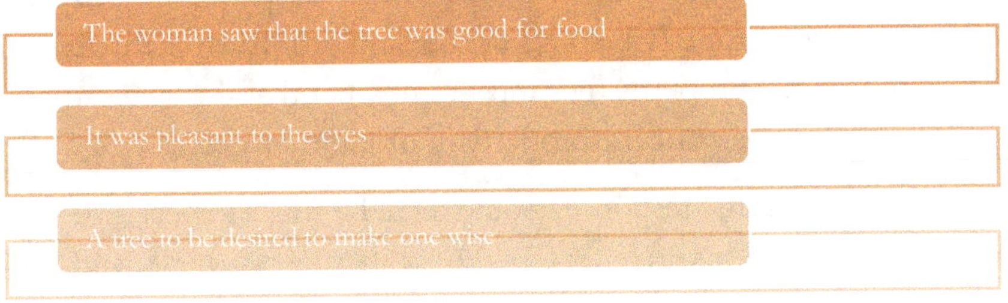

1.5 Adam and Eve recognized their error after they ate from the tree

After Adam and Eve ate, they knew something had gone wrong. They then learned that they were naked and sewed fig leaves to cover their nakedness.

Genesis 3:7

⁷And the eyes of them both were opened, and they knew that they were naked; and they sewed fig leaves together, and made themselves aprons.

One of the side effects of sin is that it makes people become naked. This happens because the protection of God is withdrawn from their lives. People often try to hide from God when they sin. However, God is a Spirit and no one can hide from him, even if they camouflage their identity.

1.6 God's visit and his civil conversation with Adam and Eve

In the cool of the day, God chose to visit Adam and Eve (Genesis 3:8). Both Adam and Eve heard God walking in the garden. Therefore, before God physically reached their specific location, they were aware of his presence.

The first conversation between them and God was a civil one. God asked Adam where he was (Genesis 3:9). This means that he was expecting to see Adam without having to ask where he was. When the landlord announces that he or she will be visiting the property for inspection, then the tenant is expected to be present when the landlord arrives. The tenant should not be hiding in the property given to him or her, since the property belongs to the landlord. Even if the tenant tries to hide in the property, they must remember that the landlord has keys to access all parts of the property in order to inspect it.

Adam provided a true response about where he was. However, he was nervous in his response. He let God know that he was afraid and had chosen to hide himself (Genesis 3:10). God then asked Adam another important question (Genesis 3:11). This time around, it was a pointed question about the restriction that God had given to Adam. Adam could not beat around the bush this time; he had to provide the correct answer, since God was specific with his second question.

In Adam's attempts to answer the second question from God, he included Eve in the response. However, in God's first two questions for Adam, he referred only to Adam, not to Eve. God was deliberate in his conversation with Adam, so he never included Eve, as he remembered that his clear line of communication was through Adam.

Adam's response showed that he had nothing to do picking the fruit from the tree that was in the middle of the garden. He was clear that it was Eve who gave him the fruit to eat. Therefore, we see that Adam wanted to take himself away from the situation. Take note, Adam clearly made it known that he did not ask Eve to eat from the tree, but rather, she gave him the fruit to eat. This meant that he did not request to be a part of the problem, but nevertheless, he did not refuse his wife's offer to him. With Adam's skillful presentation, he expected God not to punish him.

Since Adam mentioned Eve to God, then God asked Eve to provide her explanation (Genesis 3:13). Eve provided her own answer, but she blamed the serpent. So, instead of God having to deal with one person, he had to deal with two persons and one reptile to address the first sin. Their responses were long and complex, looking like never-ending steps.

God never asked the serpent for a response, since he knew the serpent to be a deceiver. Therefore, God took immediate actions against all parties that were involved in the first sin.

Genesis 3:8-13

[8] And they heard the voice of the LORD God walking in the garden in the cool of the day: and Adam and his wife hid from the presence of the LORD God amongst the trees of the garden. [9] And the LORD God called unto Adam, and said unto him, Where art thou? [10] And he said, I heard thy voice in the garden, and I was afraid, because I was naked; and I hid myself. [11] And he said, Who told thee that thou wast naked? Hast thou eaten of the tree, whereof I commanded thee that thou shouldest not eat? [12] And the man said, The woman whom thou gavest to be with me, she gave me of the tree, and I did eat.

[13] And the LORD God said unto the woman, What is this that thou hast done? And the woman said, The serpent beguiled me, and I did eat.

1.7 God's response to the first sin

After the first sin occurred, God's first response was to institute sanctions for all the guilty parties. No one was spared, since God does not have favorites. As a good parent, God got down to the bottom of the story. He knew of all the guilty parties before he instituted his sanctions. God addressed the problem from the very first date when it occurred, since he did not want sin to continue in the garden.

Genesis 3:14-19

[14] And the LORD God said unto the serpent, Because thou hast done this, thou art cursed above all cattle, and above every beast of the field; upon thy belly shalt thou go, and dust shalt thou eat all the days of thy life: [15] And I will put enmity between thee and the woman, and between thy seed and her seed; it shall bruise thy head, and thou shalt bruise his heel.

[16] Unto the woman he said, I will greatly multiply thy sorrow and thy conception; in sorrow thou shalt bring forth children; and thy desire shall be to thy husband, and he shall rule over thee. [17] And unto Adam he said, Because thou hast hearkened unto the voice of thy wife, and hast eaten of the tree, of which I commanded thee, saying, Thou shalt not eat of it: cursed is the ground for thy sake; in sorrow shalt thou eat of it all the days of thy life; [18] Thorns also and thistles shall it bring forth to thee; and thou shalt eat the herb of the field; [19] In the sweat of thy face shalt thou eat bread, till thou return unto the ground; for out of it wast thou has taken: for dust thou art, and unto dust shalt thou return.

Figure 3. God's sanctions against the serpent, Eve, and Adam (Genesis 3:14-19)

God ensured that each party to the first sin was sanctioned. The sanctions they received were permanent and affected future generations. Even after they died, their offspring would have to endure those sanctions.

Figure 4. Sequence of parties involved in the first sin and how God handed down his sanctions

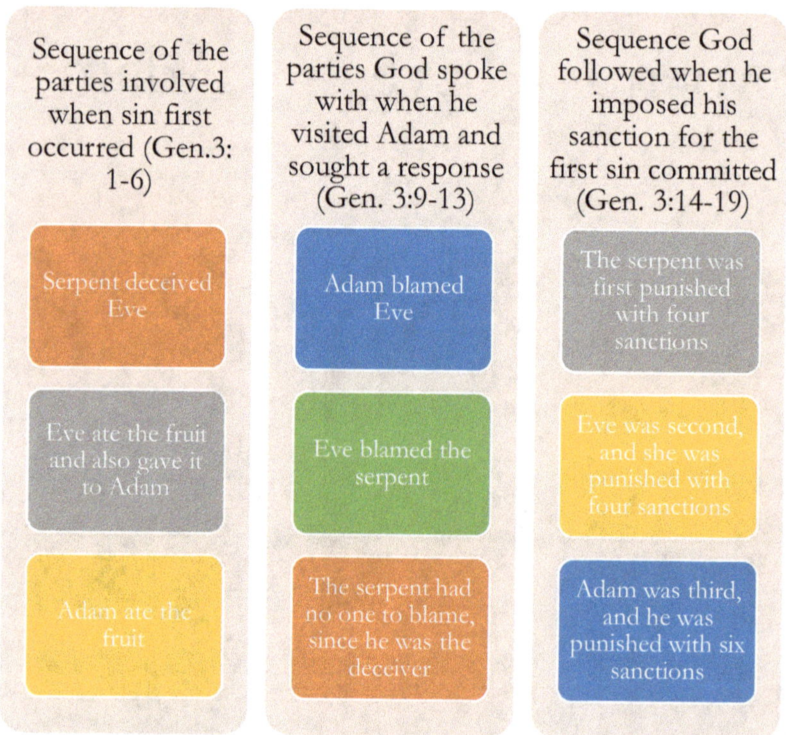

In each of the three sections in the illustration above, Eve found herself in the middle. When God came down in the cool of the day, he first spoke with Adam, and then Adam blamed Eve and Eve blamed the serpent. When God was ready to impose his sanctions, he started off with the last guilty party, in the reverse order from how God found out what caused Adam to be hiding. On this occasion, it was the serpent first, and then God imposed sanctions on Eve and finally Adam. God never dealt with Eve first, since she was always in the center of the situation.

More sanctions were imposed on Adam than the others, since he should have known better. Adam was the first person God made and the first person to whom God gave the specific instruction. When Eve gave the fruit to Adam, God expected Adam to refuse it, but instead, he ate, and that resulted in both of them sinning against God.

1.8 God's love for his creation

Although God drove Adam and Eve from the garden of Eden, he exercised mercy on them. He ensured that they had clothes as their eyes were opened and they were relocated from the garden of Eden.

Genesis 3:21-24

[21] Unto Adam also and to his wife did the LORD God make coats of skins, and clothed them. [22] And the LORD God said, Behold, the man is become as one of us, to know good and evil: and now, lest he put forth his hand, and take also of the tree of life, and eat, and live for ever: [23] Therefore the LORD God sent him forth from the garden of Eden, to till the ground from whence he was taken. [24] So he drove out the man; and he placed at the east of the garden of Eden Cherubims, and a flaming sword which turned every way, to keep the way of the tree of life.

2. Jesus existed before Adam

Before Adam was born, Jesus existed. When heaven and earth were created on the first day, Jesus already existed. An important question persons may want to know is, where was Jesus then, and what form was he in?

2.1 Jesus was in the spirit before the world existed

No one could have touched Jesus before his birth, or even seen him. Before Adam and Eve existed, from the first day of creation, Jesus was already there, but in the spirit form.

In the beginning when God said "Let us make man in our image," this was an indication that Jesus was already there in the spirit form (Genesis 1:26). When Jesus was born, he was made available in the flesh form, such that he could be seen and touched by people.

> **Genesis 1:26**
>
> [26] And God said, Let us make man in our image, after our likeness: and let them have dominion over the fish of the sea, and over the fowl of the air, and over the cattle, and over all the earth, and over every creeping thing that creepeth upon the earth.

The birth of Jesus allowed him to be on the earth and walk among people. He was willing to change form so that he could feel what humans feel. He changed form so that he could die for the sins of the world and reconcile man unto God. Thanks be to Jesus for making a great sacrifice to become human and dying for the sins of all humans.

2.2 Jesus testified that he existed before humanity

If persons have any doubts about whether Jesus existed before heaven and earth were created, Jesus put that matter to rest. In the first chapter of the Gospel of John, Jesus immediately brought to everyone's attention that he existed before the first day of creation.

John 1:1-5

[1] In the beginning was the Word, and the Word was with God, and the Word was God. [2] The same was in the beginning with God. [3] All things were made by him; and without him was not any thing made that was made. [4] In him was life; and the life was the light of men. [5] And the light shineth in darkness; and the darkness comprehended it not.

Wherever "Word" is used in John 1:1, it refers to Jesus. Therefore, "Word" can be replaced with "Jesus" in this verse, thus showing that Jesus predates Adam and Eve, as well as the first day of creation. So, when Jesus walked on the earth, he did so in his physical form, but he moved over the earth many times in the spirit before he came to earth.

As Jesus walked on the earth, he spoke in parables. In John 1:1-2, he indicates that he existed before, because he says that the "Word" was in the beginning with God and that nothing was made without him (John 1:3). In Jesus was life, and the life was light of men (John 1:4). So, when people look for hope, they find it, since Jesus is that light that everyone needs.

John 8:12

[12] Then spake Jesus again unto them, saying, I am the light of the world: he that followeth me shall not walk in darkness, but shall have the light of life.

There was no need for Jesus to boast about himself. He spoke the truth about himself, but many persons did not understand that he existed before anything was created.

2.3 Jesus said that he and the Father are one

This dates back to Genesis 1:26, as we see that Jesus knew many things about the Father because he was with the Father before Adam and Eve were created. When Jesus presented information about the Father, he was confident in his presentation. He knew what he was talking about because he and the Father are one.

John 10:30

[30] I and my Father are one.

While many religious leaders argued with him when he spoke of his close relationship with the Father, only Jesus knew what he was talking about. Some religious leaders thought Jesus was blaspheming, but he was one with the Father.

3. Jesus came for sinners

As Jesus continued his earthly ministry, he dwelled among many sinners, interacted with them, and even ate with them. His actions caused many religious people to question him. They did not perceive him to be the Savior, since he was often seen communicating with sinners.

The men Jesus called to be his disciples were sinners. Jesus spent time healing sick people. He listened to their concerns and provided solutions. Instead of going to an established place of worship, Jesus often went to places where sinners were. Most times when Jesus visited the temple, he rebuked the religious leaders.

Jesus always demonstrated a hatred for sin, but he loved sinners. He knew that he had come for sinners and not for the righteous people (Mark 2:17). Jesus hates sins, but he wants to save the sinners.

Mark 2:13-17

[13] And he went forth again by the sea side; and all the multitude resorted unto him, and he taught them. [14] And as he passed by, he saw Levi the son of Alpheus sitting at the receipt of custom, and said unto him, Follow me. And he arose and followed him. [15] And it came to pass, that, as Jesus sat at meat in his house, many publicans and sinners sat also together with Jesus and his disciples: for there were many, and they followed him. [16] And when the scribes and Pharisees saw him eat with publicans and sinners, they said unto his disciples, How is it that he eateth and drinketh with publicans and sinners? [17] When Jesus heard it, he saith unto them, They that are whole have no need of the physician, but they that are sick: I came not to call the righteous, but sinners to repentance.

Levi was involved in tax collection (Mark 2:14). Jesus saw Levi and said to him, "Follow me." With that request from Jesus, Levi quickly followed him. Jesus went to Levi's house and ate with him. These actions and communication between Levi and Jesus caused the scribes and Pharisees to be concerned about Jesus' interactions with sinners (Mark 2:15-16). Jesus provided a surprising response to the scribes and Pharisees after they questioned him about associating with sinners: he let them know that he had come to call sinners (Mark 2:17). Therefore, the scribes and Pharisees ought not to question him any more about his interactions with sinners.

4. A Savior is needed

After the first sin occurred, God knew that a Savior was needed. Man could not help himself from his sin, and so God intervened and provided the solution needed.

Genesis 3:15

¹⁵ And I will put enmity between thee and the woman, and between thy seed and her seed; it shall bruise thy head, and thou shalt bruise his heel.

4.1 Does the first sin affect all humans?

Some persons argue that it was Adam and Eve who sinned. However, because of that sin, everyone is affected. No human can be excluded from Adam and Eve's sin.

Romans 3:23

²³ For all have sinned, and come short of the glory of God.

When Apostle Paul wrote to the Romans, he informed them that all have sinned. This statement was probably surprising to some of them, but the apostle was correct, since no one is righteous (Romans 3:20).

Romans 3:9-20

⁹ What then? Are we better than they? No, in no wise: for we have before proved both Jews and Gentiles, that they are all under sin; ¹⁰ As it is written, There is none righteous, no, not one: ¹¹ There is none that understandeth, there is none that seeketh after God. ¹² They are all gone out of the way, they are together become unprofitable; there is none that doeth good, no, not one.

[13] Their throat is an open sepulcher; with their tongues they have used deceit; the poison of asps is under their lips: [14] Whose mouth is full of cursing and bitterness: [15] Their feet are swift to shed blood: [16] Destruction and misery are in their ways: [17] And the way of peace have they not known: [18] There is no fear of God before their eyes.

[19] Now we know that what things soever the law saith, it saith to them who are under the law: that every mouth may be stopped, and all the world may become guilty before God. [20] Therefore by the deeds of the law there shall no flesh be justified in his sight: for by the law is the knowledge of sin.

4.2 Christ Jesus justifies the sinners

The Savior's entrance into the earth was to justify people of their sins. While everyone has sinned and missed God's mark, he still provided them with an option to be redeemed. This redemption will only be made possible through the Savior.

Romans 3:21-31

[21] But now the righteousness of God without the law is manifested, being witnessed by the law and the prophets; [22] Even the righteousness of God which is by faith of Jesus Christ unto all and upon all them that believe: for there is no difference: [23] For all have sinned, and come short of the glory of God; [24] Being justified freely by his grace through the redemption that is in Christ Jesus: [25] Whom God hath set forth to be a propitiation through faith in his blood, to declare his righteousness for the remission of sins that are past, through the forbearance of God; [26] To declare, I say, at this time his righteousness: that he might be just, and the justifier of him which believeth in Jesus.

[27] Where is boasting then? It is excluded. By what law? of works? Nay: but by the law of faith. [28] Therefore we conclude that a man is justified by faith without the deeds of the law. [29] Is

he the God of the Jews only? Is he not also of the Gentiles? Yes, of the Gentiles also: [30] Seeing it is one God, which shall justify the circumcision by faith, and uncircumcision through faith. [31] Do we then make void the law through faith? God forbid: yea, we establish the law.

4.3 Can people's good works save them?

Some persons think they do not need the Savior. Therefore, they will try to do everything possible to save themselves. However, no one is perfect, and their best efforts will never allow them to be redeemed. Jesus offers saving grace to all sinners. No one has an excuse for not being saved, once Jesus has been presented to them.

Ephesians 2:8-10

[8] For by grace are ye saved through faith; and that not of yourselves: it is the gift of God: [9] Not of works, lest any man should boast. [10] For we are his workmanship, created in Christ Jesus unto good works, which God hath before ordained that we should walk in them.

5. Jesus came to reconcile man to God

Before sin existed, man had a good relationship with the Father. But after man sinned, that relationship and trust was fractured. It is never God's intention to keep himself away from his creation.

Jesus came to bridge the gap between man and God. He had to make a sacrifice that no one else was worthy to make.

Ephesians 2:11-22

[11] Wherefore remember, that ye being in time past Gentiles in the flesh, who are called Uncircumcision by that which is called the Circumcision in the flesh made by hands; [12] That at that time ye were without Christ, being aliens from the commonwealth of Israel, and strangers from the covenants of promise, having no hope, and without God in the world: [13] But now in Christ Jesus ye who sometimes were far off are made nigh by the blood of Christ.

[14] For he is our peace, who hath made both one, and hath broken down the middle wall of partition between us; [15] Having abolished in his flesh the enmity, even the law of commandments contained in ordinances; for to make in himself of twain one new man, so making peace; [16] And that he might reconcile both unto God in one body by the cross, having slain the enmity thereby: [17] And came and preached peace to you which were afar off, and to them that were nigh. [18] For through him we both have access by one Spirit unto the Father.

[19] Now therefore ye are no more strangers and foreigners, but fellowcitizens with the saints, and of the household of God; [20] And are built upon the foundation of the apostles and prophets, Jesus Christ himself being the chief corner stone; [21] In whom all the building fitly framed together groweth unto an holy temple in the Lord: [22] In whom ye also are builded together for an habitation of God through the Spirit.

The Apostle Paul presents a great remainder to believers that Christ came to reconcile them (Ephesians 2:16). It took the life of Jesus for man to be reconciled to God. Jesus did not come to the earth on a vacation, but to do everything necessary within his brief earthly ministry to give man the opportunity to have sweet fellowship with the Father.

2 Corinthians 5:18-19

[18] And all things are of God, who hath reconciled us to himself by Jesus Christ, and hath given to us the ministry of reconciliation; [19] To wit, that God was in Christ, reconciling the world unto himself, not imputing their trespasses unto them; and hath committed unto us the word of reconciliation.

Apostle Paul presents another good reason for Christ's visit to the earth, stating that God reconciled the world to himself through Christ (2 Corinthians 5:19). This shows that God always wanted to redeem man, despite the sin of Adam.

When Adam sinned, Christ knew about it, because he was there before the world existed (Colossians 1:15-18). So, when Christ was sent to the earth, he knew exactly what he needed to do to reconcile the world to the Father (Colossians 1:19-23).

Colossians 1:15-23

[15] Who is the image of the invisible God, the firstborn of every creature: [16] For by him were all things created, that are in heaven, and that are in earth, visible and invisible, whether they be thrones, or dominions, or principalities, or powers: all

things were created by him, and for him: [17] And he is before all things, and by him all things consist. [18] And he is the head of the body, the church: who is the beginning, the firstborn from the dead; that in all things he might have the preeminence.

[19] For it pleased the Father that in him should all fulness dwell; [20] And, having made peace through the blood of his cross, by him to reconcile all things unto himself; by him, I say, whether they be things in earth, or things in heaven. [21] And you, that were sometime alienated and enemies in your mind by wicked works, yet now hath he reconciled [22] In the body of his flesh through death, to present you holy and unblameable and unreproveable in his sight: [23] If ye continue in the faith grounded and settled, and be not moved away from the hope of the gospel, which ye have heard, and which was preached to every creature which is under heaven; whereof I Paul am made a minister.

Persons must accept Christ into their lives and live for him. Salvation is available to all. No one will be discriminated against when they seek Christ to forgive them of their sins. Whether a person is a Jew or Gentile, the Lord is willing to save them. There is no age or gender barrier preventing a person from seeking forgiveness from the Lord.

6. Jesus' birth, status, and purpose prophesied

It is well known that Jesus is not an ordinary man. His earthly ministry was foretold many centuries ago.

He is so important that many details about his birth and purpose were revealed in advance. Indeed, when he walked on the earth, he confirmed the prophesies that were spoken about him.

6.1 Unto us a child is given

Isaiah 9:6 provides a strong statement about Jesus, showing readers that a son is given unto the entire universe.

Isaiah 9:6-7

[6] For unto us a child is born, unto us a son is given: and the government shall be upon his shoulder: and his name shall be called Wonderful, Counsellor, The mighty God, The everlasting Father, and The Prince of Peace. [7] Of the increase of his government and peace there shall be no end, upon the throne of David, and upon his kingdom, to order it, and to establish it with judgment and with justice from henceforth even for ever. The zeal of the LORD of hosts will perform this.

6.2 Came to the earth as a baby

Before Jesus came to the earth, his status was already known. He was a great leader, yet he operated in simplicity. He did not ignore the less fortunate. Many low-level persons felt comfortable coming to him because he was always approachable, and when they left his presence, their lives were better.

Table 1. Jesus' gender and leadership roles were foretold (Isaiah 9:6-7)

What the scripture prophesied about Jesus	Explanation
For unto us a child is born	Jesus came into this world as a child. He was born for the benefit of the world and not for the benefit of Mary and Joseph. The first Adam was not born as a child, since he was created by God from the dust of the earth as an adult. The prophecy about Jesus was clear that he would be born as a baby and grow through all the stages of human development. Jesus did not skip any stage in human development, so he is acquainted with the challenges that people will go through.
Unto us a son is given	The gender of Jesus was foretold. This child that would be born to save the world was to be a man child. This child is given unto humanity to save them from their sins.
The government shall be upon his shoulder	Jesus was never a politician. He never ran for any office or political leadership position, but he was entrusted with a leadership role even before he was born. After Jesus came to this world, he would become the new leader. He had the ability to naturally lead many persons (including politicians, business people, firemen,

	religious leaders, etc.). Many persons followed him because he was a great leader. He understood the needs of the people and always met their needs. As a leader, he was influential to everyone he met.
His name shall be called Wonderful	Indeed, his name shall be called Wonderful. When he came to the earth, he would wow the people with his performance and wisdom. Many persons followed him, as his name made a great impact in their lives. Unto this day, demons tremble at the name of Jesus. When many persons die, their names are forgotten; however, when Jesus died, his name continued and will continue forever. Jesus does not need anyone to make him great, since he was born with greatness inside of him.
Counsellor	There are some leaders who cannot counsel people, but Jesus was a leader with this ability. He was a good listener and listened to the people's problems. Even children could get his attention because of his heart for people. Jesus brought his Father's counsel to the earth so that everyone can be given a fair hearing for whatever is affecting them. Children also have free access to go to him and state their problems, and he will listen to them and provide them with appropriate answers. He also counseled religious leaders.

The mighty God	Jesus is God the Son. He is also mighty. He has great power and performed miracles as a mighty God. In Jesus dwells the fullness of the Godhead.
The everlasting Father	Abraham was called "father of nations." Jesus is not only a father, but he is a father who will live forever. All the great fathers that the world knew are dead, but Jesus lives on beyond the grave. When many great fathers die, their names fade away. Many great fathers cannot do anything to help their offspring after their death. However, Jesus still lives in the hearts of everyone who accepts him. Jesus, as a father, is still there to hear and answer the request of everyone who asks of him.
The Prince of Peace	The title of "Prince of Peace" shows that Jesus is the Son, so he is a Prince and his Father is the King. Jesus was born with royalty in his blood. Before he was born, he already had rulership over the kingdom. Jesus did not have to wait for some monarch in his family to die for him to inherit the kingdom, but he preached about his kingdom at an early stage in his ministry. When many monarchs have power, they can either bless people or hurt people. However, Jesus, the Prince of Peace, only plans to bring peace to the earth and to the lives of people. Throughout the earth, he preached his message in peace and reminded the disciples that if people rejected the gospel,

	the disciples must preach to others who will listen to them. Jesus taught his followers to be peacemakers.
Of the increase of his government and peace there shall be no end	The name of Jesus preceded him. Even after his death, his government continues. Jesus is the only man who, after his death, is still preached about and saves those who come to him. His kingdom is not decreasing but increasing. His span of control did not cease at his death but began to spread faster. When many politicians and governments are having wars, Jesus continues to spread peace throughout the earth. After Jesus ascended, he reminded believers to go and teach all nations whatever they observed that he did and whatever he stands for.
Upon the throne of David	David could not build the first temple of God because of his sin. However, God told King David that he would make his name great. Therefore, God directed the birth of Jesus through the lineage of King David. Unto this day, many persons ascribe the works that Jesus did to a great leader, King David. Jesus did not come to destroy the throne of David, but to build on that throne.
Upon his kingdom	Jesus taught about the kingdom of God throughout his time on the earth. The

	kingdoms of many leaders will cease, but the kingdom of God remains forever. Jesus taught about a new kingdom that people were not aware of, but many are now benefiting from this new kingdom.
To order it	As a leader, Jesus has the ability to order how his kingdom operates and how people will enter it. No one can enter the kingdom of God without passing through Jesus. Jesus reminds persons that he is the way to the Father and that no one will access the Father except through him. The rules of the kingdom of God are not established by man but by the Lord.
To establish it with judgment and with justice from henceforth even for ever	The kingdom of God is not governed by the judgment and justice of men. It can be seen in many nations that the justice system is not perfect, as many persons who do wrong things are rewarded as though they have done the correct thing. However, with the kingdom of God, those who do the wrong things will be punished and those who do the right things will be rewarded. Jesus is also willing to forgive everyone who has sinned. Since everyone has sinned and fallen short of God's expectation, they need Jesus in order to enter the kingdom of God under his leadership.
The zeal of the Lord of hosts will perform this	The leadership and reign of Jesus was a well-coordinated event of God. Although persons wanted to prevent the birth of Jesus

and then to prevent him from fulfilling his assignment, they could not stop him, since God predestined the coming of Jesus and his ministry. Whatever the Lord has promised, he will bring it to pass, since nothing and no one can stop God from executing his plans.

As Jesus preached that the kingdom of heaven is at hand, he had a kingdom mandate, and he executed that mandate well. He knew of the kingdom that he was speaking about.

7. The birth of Jesus

Before Mary gave birth to baby Jesus, he already existed in the spirit. God saw the need for his Son to be on the earth, in the flesh, so he wanted to make sure that Jesus came to the earth through human means, with the exception of fertilization. Therefore, God chose Mary to carry the fetus that would change believers' walk with the Lord.

Whatever the Father promises, he will cause it to happen. Due to the first sin, God automatically arranged to send his Son on earth in human form to save everyone. Jesus came to the earth as a baby and not as an adult, so he went through all the things humans have to endure. The one difference is that Mary's fertilization did not occur due to the biological process of sperm and egg; instead, God caused her to be pregnant before Joseph knew her.

Since Jesus was born as a baby, there was a need for parents to be involved in the process. God selected two competent persons to be considered the earthly parents of Jesus. While these two persons were not aware that they were going to be selected to be earthly parents for Jesus, they both provided whatever support they could. Mary doubted her ability to be the chosen vessel to carry Jesus for nine months in the womb. Joseph was considering whether he should still proceed with the marriage, but the angel spoke to him, and he decided to accept Mary to be his wife.

7.1 A virgin will give birth

God ensured that he chose a virgin to be the carrier of baby Jesus. This was not an accident, as it was already prophesied that a virgin will give birth.

Isaiah 7:14

[14] Therefore the Lord himself shall give you a sign; Behold, a virgin shall conceive, and bear a son, and shall call his name Immanuel.

From Isaiah 7:14, it is clear that a virgin would give birth. The gender of the child was also known, and importantly, so was the name of the child. Therefore, God planned the entire event of Jesus' birth.

7.2 Virgin Mary became pregnant

Mary was pregnant while Joseph was contemplating whether to take her to be his wife. This situation caused much unease for Joseph.

While Mary and Joseph were espoused to each other, they did not engage in sex (Matthew 1:18), so it surprised Joseph to understand that his wife was pregnant (Matthew 1:19-20). Nevertheless, the angel spoke to Joseph, and he agreed with God that he would keep Mary.

Matthew 1:18-24

[18] Now the birth of Jesus Christ was on this wise: When as his mother Mary was espoused to Joseph, before they came together, she was found with child of the Holy Ghost. [19] Then Joseph her husband, being a just man, and not willing to make her a public example, was minded to put her away privily. [20] But while he thought on these things, behold, the angel of the LORD appeared unto him in a dream, saying, Joseph, thou son of David, fear not to take unto thee Mary thy wife: for that which is conceived in her is of the Holy Ghost. [21] And she shall bring forth a son, and thou shalt call his name JESUS: for he shall save his people from their sins. [22] Now all this was done, that it might be fulfilled which was spoken of the Lord by the prophet, saying, [23] Behold, a virgin shall be with child, and shall bring forth a son, and they shall call his name Emmanuel, which being interpreted is, God with us. [24] Then Joseph being raised from sleep did as the angel of the Lord had bidden him, and took unto him his wife.

The angel spoke to Joseph and told him of the gender of the child. In those days, there was no equipment to determine a baby's gender before birth, but God knew the gender of the child and made that information known to his parents. The name of the child was also told to Joseph by the angel, and Joseph accepted that name.

Figure 5. What contributed to Joseph's decision to accept Mary as his wife?

God has control over all humans. While Joseph might have had other views about whether to accept Mary to be his wife, he was placed into a deep sleep (Matthew 1:24), and when he awoke from his sleep, he agreed with God's plans.

7.3 Many generations were selected and preserved for the birth of Jesus

God preserved many generations so that Jesus would enter this world through two important humans. Each generation played a critical role in contributing to God's plan that he told Abraham, as well as the covenant God had with King David. While each generation leading up to the birth of Jesus was imperfect, God used them in different ways.

Matthew 1:1-17

[1]The book of the generation of Jesus Christ, the son of David, the son of Abraham. [2]Abraham begat Isaac; and Isaac begat Jacob; and Jacob begat Judas and his brethren; [3]And Judas begat Phares and Zara of Thamar; and Phares begat Esrom; and Esrom begat Aram; [4]And Aram begat Aminadab; and Aminadab begat Naasson; and Naasson begat Salmon; [5]And Salmon begat Booz of Rachab; and Booz begat Obed of Ruth; and Obed begat Jesse; [6]And Jesse begat David the king; and David the king begat Solomon of her that had been the wife of Urias;

[7]And Solomon begat Roboam; and Roboam begat Abia; and Abia begat Asa; [8]And Asa begat Josaphat; and Josaphat begat Joram; and Joram begat Ozias; [9]And Ozias begat Joatham; and Joatham begat Achaz; and Achaz begat Ezekias; [10]And Ezekias begat Manasses; and Manasses begat Amon; and Amon begat Josias; [11]And Josias begat Jechonias and his brethren, about the time they were carried away to Babylon:

[12]And after they were brought to Babylon, Jechonias begat Salathiel; and Salathiel begat Zorobabel; [13]And Zorobabel begat Abiud; and Abiud begat Eliakim; and Eliakim begat Azor; [14]And Azor begat Sadoc; and Sadoc begat Achim; and Achim begat Eliud; [15]And Eliud begat Eleazar; and Eleazar begat Matthan; and Matthan begat Jacob; [16]And Jacob begat Joseph the husband of Mary, of whom was born Jesus, who is called Christ.

[17]So all the generations from Abraham to David are fourteen generations; and from David until the carrying away into Babylon are fourteen generations; and from the carrying away into Babylon unto Christ are fourteen generations.

Through history, God had a redemption plan, and that redemption plan materialized through Jesus. Many generations played critical roles in fulfilling God's plan for his Son to have an earthly ministry.

8. Herod could not stop Jesus' birth

During Mary's pregnancy, Herod was king. There were certain signs that Jesus was going to be born, and this troubled the mind of King Herod because Jesus would have great authority over humanity, according to Isaiah 9:6-7. Therefore, King Herod tried many things to prevent the plan of God from happening. However, no one can stop God's plan.

King Herod did not want another king to be born. Jesus came with authority to reign on the earth and in heaven. Jesus was never obsessed with power, but he executed his assignment on the earth with simplicity and excellence.

King Herod was deceptive in his plans to end Jesus' life. But while Herod was planning his next move, God was already ahead of him.

Table 2. Jesus' birth and King Herod's deceptive actions (Matthew 2:1-23)

Scripture	Explanation
¹Now when Jesus was born in Bethlehem of Judaea in the days of Herod the king, behold, there came wise men from the east to Jerusalem	Jesus was born in Bethlehem, which fulfilled the prophecy that was spoken about his place of birth (Micah 5:2). Bethlehem was the ancestral home of King David, and Jesus was born through King David's lineage.

Jesus was born in the time when Herod was king over Judea.

The three wise men traveled from the east to Jerusalem. This was not a coincidence but allowed the will of God to be fulfilled.

The three wise men (philosophers or astrologers) inquired about the birth of Jesus. These men understood times and seasons, and they already knew that Jesus was born King of the Jews. It may appear strange to some persons that Jesus was very young and could not talk, yet the three wise men already knew his status in society.

The only guide for the three wise men was a star that shone in the east. There were many stars in the sky, but God allowed them to see this significant star, as it provided direction to them about the location of Jesus.

The three wise men knew of Jesus' superior reign, so they came to worship him (Isaiah 60:1-6).

2 Saying, Where is he that is born King of the Jews? for we have seen his star in the east, and are come to worship him

	Jesus was born King of the Jews, yet his parents had no royal status. This all became possible because God was in total control over this miraculous birth.
3 When Herod the king had heard these things, he was troubled, and all Jerusalem with him	King Herod was worried when he heard that another king was born and that this new king would be worshipped. This news must have troubled King Herod, since more attention would be paid to Jesus and less to King Herod. Not only was King Herod troubled, but so were the people of Jerusalem. Herod was an influential leader and did not want any other king to reign while he was on his throne. Herod operated like a narcissist, wanting to be in control and to be praised.
4 And when he had gathered all the chief priests and scribes of the people together, he demanded of them where Christ should be born	King Herod was ready to take action against the new king that was born "King of the Jews." He wanted to hear from the religious leaders (chief priests and scribes) about the birth and location of Jesus. King Herod did not ask them gently but demanded

	answers about where Christ was born, since he thought that they must know something about this prophecy being fulfilled.
⁵ And they said unto him, In Bethlehem of Judaea: for thus it is written by the prophet,	The religious leaders were honest and provided King Herod with the correct location of Jesus' birth.
⁶ And thou Bethlehem, in the land of Juda, art not the least among the princes of Juda: for out of thee shall come a Governor, that shall rule my people Israel.	God was doing something great through ordinary people (Mary and Joseph) and in an ordinary place (Bethlehem, in the land of Judea). Christ would be born as Governor and would rule the people of Israel (Isaiah 9:6-7).
⁷ Then Herod, when he had privily called the wise men, enquired of them diligently what time the star appeared.	King Herod was worried. He had already called the religious leaders to him (Matthew 2:4), and now he called the wise men. Take note, he called the wise men privately, since he did not want too many persons to know that he was inquiring about this young child who was born King of the Jews. The birth of Jesus was already making King Herod nervous. The wise men were from a different country,

so King Herod's approach to them was different.

He asked the wise men about the timing of when the star appeared. He was trying to assess the age of Jesus so that he could bring an end to the life of this upcoming king.

8 And he sent them to Bethlehem, and said, Go and search diligently for the young child; and when ye have found him, bring me word again, that I may come and worship him also.

Herod was working his strategy. He wanted to kill Jesus, so he wanted to know the exact location where Jesus was born. While King Herod used the choice words "that I may worship him also," his evil strategy was to locate Jesus and kill him. He used the word "also" because he wanted to convince the three wise men that he wanted to worship Christ like they did.

9 When they had heard the king, they departed; and, lo, the star, which they saw in the east, went before them, till it came and stood over where the young child was.

10 When they saw the star, they rejoiced with exceeding great joy.

The three wise men showed respect to King Herod as they listened to him, and then they continued their journey. God was working through the three wise men. While they were having discussions with King Herod, the star remained in position and continue to move when they were ready. This star was no ordinary star, since it came and stood where the young child was. The hands of God were working through this entire process, and God's prophecy had to be fulfilled.

The three wise men rejoiced with exceeding great joy, since the star was miraculously guiding them throughout their journey.

11 And when they were come into the house, they saw the young child with Mary his mother, and fell down, and worshipped him: and when they had opened their treasures, they presented unto him gifts; gold, and frankincense and myrrh.

The three wise men did as they planned: they worshipped the King of the Jews. These three wise men did not come empty handed but carried precious gifts with them. It is clear that this was a planned journey for these three wise men.

At this time, Jesus was still a child and was with his earthly parents.

God continued to be good, as he directed the three wise men to the exact location of Jesus as the star guided them.

12 And being warned of God in a dream that they should not return to Herod, they departed into their own country another way.

While King Herod met with the three wise men privately and expected that they would return to him with the exact location of Christ's birth, God spoke to these three wise men, and they departed to their own country by another route. God was already at work and was protecting his Son, Jesus.

13 And when they were departed, behold, the angel of the Lord appeareth to Joseph in a dream, saying, Arise, and take the young child and his mother, and flee into Egypt, and be thou there until I bring thee word: for Herod will seek the young child to destroy him.

This is the second time that Joseph received a dream and was spoken to by an angel. The first dream was for him to take Mary as his wife (Matthew 1:20-22), and the second dream was for him to take his family into Egypt (Matthew 2:13). God provided a clear warning to Joseph to stay in Egypt. Joseph was already informed that King Herod wanted to kill the child. God is always ahead of the enemy, but believers need to listen to God and follow his instructions.

14 When he arose, he took the young child and his mother by night, and departed into Egypt:

Joseph was working along with God's direction. Joseph took his family out of Bethlehem by night so that no one would know where they fled to. God will always outfox evil people and Satan. If Joseph and his family had gone to Egypt by day, then persons would have seen when they were traveling and know of their new location. At night, there would be little visibility without the use of bright lights.

15 And was there until the death of Herod: that it might be fulfilled which was spoken of the Lord by the prophet, saying, Out of Egypt have I called my son.

God protected and provided for Joseph and his family while they were in a strange country. While Joseph may have thought that he was accidentally sent to a strange country, it was the country that the Lord wanted in order to fulfill his prophecy (Hosea 11:1). God had all events and locations synchronized, and King Herod could not do anything to stop the will of God.

16 Then Herod, when he saw that he was mocked of the wise men, was exceeding wroth, and sent forth, and slew all the children that were in Bethlehem, and in all the coasts thereof, from two years old and under, according to the time which he had diligently inquired of the wise men.

King Herod was furious. He knew that because a certain amount of time had passed and the three wise men had not returned, that meant they would not be returning to him. Because the three wise men were not from his country, he could not put any sanction on them for violating his request.

King Herod then decided to commit genocide. He instructed that all children two years and under be killed. The areas that he identified were within the area where Jesus was. However, while King Herod carried out his mischief, God had already arranged for Jesus to be in Egypt with his family.

¹⁷ Then was fulfilled that which was spoken by Jeremiah the prophet, saying,

¹⁸ In Rama was there a voice heard, lamentation, and weeping, and great mourning, Rachel weeping for her children, and would not be comforted, because they are not.

King Herod killed many innocent lives, yet it fulfilled a prophecy that was spoken in the days of Jeremiah (Jeremiah 31:15). Although King Herod killed so many young children, he could not kill Jesus, as God had already protected Jesus by sending him to Egypt.

¹⁹ But when Herod was dead, behold, an angel of the Lord appeareth in a dream to Joseph in Egypt,

²⁰ Saying, Arise, and take the young child and his mother, and go into the land of Israel: for they are dead which sought the young child's life.

This was the third time that Joseph received a dream with specific instructions. Joseph was aware that King Herod had died, and so it was a good time to move from his temporary location in Egypt.

²¹ And he arose, and took the young child and his mother, and came into the land of Israel.

Like many other persons, Joseph was afraid to return to his country because a son of King Herod was ruling the country. He fled to Nazareth,

²² **But when he heard that Archelaus did reign in Judaea in the room of his father Herod, he was afraid to go thither: notwithstanding, being warned of God in a dream, he turned aside into the parts of Galilee:**

²³ **And he came and dwelt in a city called Nazareth: that it might be fulfilled which was spoken by the prophets, He shall be called a Nazarene.**

returning to the place where the angel had met with Mary (Luke 1:26-27).

God never aborted his plan for the birth of Jesus, despite King Herod's great attempts to end the life of baby Jesus. The birth of Jesus was planned long before King Herod existed.

9. Jesus' death was predicted

Many persons wished that Jesus would live on the earth forever. However, his earthly ministry was short. He fulfilled his assignment, and then it was time for him to take his exit from the earth.

The actions of Judas were not a surprise to Jesus. In fact, Judas was only fulfilling God's plans. No one can put a believer to death unless God gives permission for them to do so. On many occasions, Jesus told people that his death was coming.

9.1 Jesus wanted to know if the disciples knew who he was

To test the disciples, Jesus asked them one question (Matthew 16:13). This was not a multiple-choice question, but rather an essay question. He wanted to hear from them what they knew about him and his earthly purpose. After attempts by some of the disciples to discuss who Jesus was, only Apostle Peter provided the correct answer (Matthew 16:13-20). Since the correct answer was provided, Jesus knew that his mission was near completion.

It is always important for leaders to ask their immediate support staff to evaluate them or provide an assessment of how they perceive their leaders are doing. The response may not always be favorable, but it is important to receive evaluations from those who walk closely with the leaders.

9.2 Jesus predicted his death for the first time

After Peter provided the correct answer about who Jesus is, he explained to them that he must go to Jerusalem (Matthew 16:21). This was a clear indication that he knew his time on the earth was about to end. He also knew the community where his death would take place. Jesus voluntarily surrendered to death because he had fulfilled his earthly assignments. Jesus told the disciples not to tell others about who he is (Matthew 16:20).

Matthew 16:13-28

[13] When Jesus came into the coasts of Caesarea Philippi, he asked his disciples, saying, who do men say that I the Son of man am? [14] And they said, some say that thou art John the Baptist: some, Elias; and others, Jeremias, or one of the prophets. [15] He saith unto them, But whom say ye that I am? [16] And Simon Peter answered and said, Thou art the Christ, the Son of the living God.

[17] And Jesus answered and said unto him, Blessed art thou, Simon Barjona: for flesh and blood hath not revealed it unto thee, but my Father which is in heaven. [18] And I say also unto thee, That thou art Peter, and upon this rock I will build my church; and the gates of hell shall not prevail against it. [19] And I will give unto thee the keys of the kingdom of heaven: and whatsoever thou shalt bind on earth shall be bound in heaven: and whatsoever thou shalt loose on earth shall be loosed in heaven. [20] Then charged he his disciples that they should tell no man that he was Jesus the Christ.

[21] From that time forth began Jesus to shew unto his disciples, how that he must go unto Jerusalem, and suffer many things of the elders and chief priests and scribes, and be killed, and be raised again the third day. [22] Then Peter took him, and began to rebuke him, saying, be it far from thee, Lord: this shall not be unto thee. [23] But he turned, and said unto Peter, Get thee behind me, Satan: thou art an offence unto me: for thou savourest not the things that be of God, but those that be of men.

[24] Then said Jesus unto his disciples, If any man will come after me, let him deny himself, and take up his cross, and follow me. [25] For whosoever will save his life shall lose it: and whosoever

will lose his life for my sake shall find it. [26] For what is a man profited, if he shall gain the whole world, and lose his own soul? or what shall a man give in exchange for his soul? [27] For the Son of man shall come in the glory of his Father with his angels; and then he shall reward every man according to his works. [28] Verily I say unto you, there be some standing here, which shall not taste of death, till they see the Son of man coming in his kingdom.

While Peter was upset that Jesus was going to die, it was necessary for Jesus to die for sinners (Matthew 16:22-28). The disciples were well informed of the punishment Jesus would have to endure before he died, since he told them what to expect (Matthew 16:21).

9.3 Jesus predicted his death a second time

Peter was angry that his master was going to die (Matthew 16:22). However, Jesus was prepared for death, since he knew he had come to die for the sins of the world.

On a second occasion, Jesus informed the disciples of his death. This caused more worries for them, but Jesus was committed to the cause for which he came.

Luke 9:43-50

[43] And they were all amazed at the mighty power of God. But while they wondered every one at all things which Jesus did, he said unto his disciples, [44] Let these sayings sink down into your ears: for the Son of man shall be delivered into the hands of men. [45] But they understood not this saying, and it was hid from them, that they perceived it not: and they feared to ask him of that saying.

[46] Then there arose a reasoning among them, which of them should be greatest. [47] And Jesus, perceiving the thought of their heart, took a child, and set him by him, [48] And said unto them, whosoever shall receive this child in my name receiveth me: and whosoever shall receive me receiveth him that sent me: for

he that is least among you all, the same shall be great. [49] And John answered and said, Master, we saw one casting out devils in thy name; and we forbad him, because he followeth not with us. [50] And Jesus said unto him, forbid him not: for he that is not against us is for us.

9.4 Jesus predicted his death for the third time

If the disciples had not heard Jesus on the first two occasions, he reminded them of his death for a third time. He ensured that those who were closest to him were well informed of his death, so that it would not be a surprise to them (Mark 10:32).

Mark 10:32-34

[32] And they were in the way going up to Jerusalem; and Jesus went before them: and they were amazed; and as they followed, they were afraid. And he took again the twelve, and began to tell them what things should happen unto him, [33] Saying, Behold, we go up to Jerusalem; and the Son of man shall be delivered unto the chief priests, and unto the scribes; and they shall condemn him to death, and shall deliver him to the Gentiles: [34] And they shall mock him, and shall scourge him, and shall spit upon him, and shall kill him: and the third day he shall rise again.

Figure 6. Jesus told his disciples of the sequence of events for his death and resurrection (Mark 10:33-34)

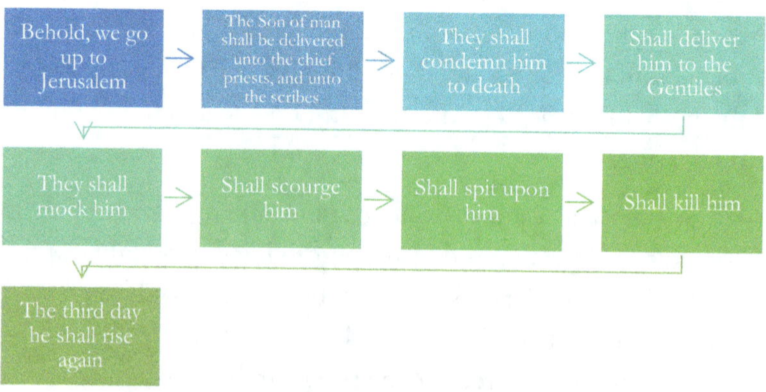

It was hard for the disciples to accept this truth, but Jesus had to tell his disciples so that when they saw the sequence of events happening, they would not be surprised. No one feels comfortable with losing a family member or friend, even if they are aware that that person is about to die and have been informed of the death. Death often creates unease for those who are still alive.

10. Events leading up to Jesus' crucifixion

As the time of Jesus' death grew closer, he spent more time with his disciples. He knew Judas would betray him, yet he did not dispose of Judas (John 13:2). Jesus knew that Judas was part of the equation that would result in his death.

The disciples' feet were washed by their leader. He remained humble and washed the feet of the adult men who followed him throughout his earthly ministry.

John 13:1-17

[1] Now before the feast of the passover, when Jesus knew that his hour was come that he should depart out of this world unto the Father, having loved his own which were in the world, he loved them unto the end. [2] And supper being ended, the devil having now put into the heart of Judas Iscariot, Simon's son, to betray him; [3] Jesus knowing that the Father had given all things into his hands, and that he was come from God, and went to God; [4] He raiseth from supper, and laid aside his garments; and took a towel, and girded himself.

[5] After that he poureth water into a bason, and began to wash the disciples' feet, and to wipe them with the towel wherewith he was girded. [6] Then cometh he to Simon Peter: and Peter saith unto him, Lord, dost thou wash my feet? [7] Jesus answered and said unto him, What I do thou knowest not now; but thou shalt know hereafter. [8] Peter saith unto him, Thou shalt never wash my feet. Jesus answered him, If I wash thee not, thou hast no part with me. [9] Simon Peter saith unto him, Lord, not my

feet only, but also my hands and my head. ¹⁰ Jesus saith to him, He that is washed needeth not save to wash his feet, but is clean every whit: and ye are clean, but not all. ¹¹ For he knew who should betray him; therefore said he, Ye are not all clean.

¹² So after he had washed their feet, and had taken his garments, and was set down again, he said unto them, Know ye what I have done to you? ¹³ Ye call me Master and Lord: and ye say well; for so I am. ¹⁴ If I then, your Lord and Master, have washed your feet; ye also ought to wash one another's feet. ¹⁵ For I have given you an example, that ye should do as I have done to you. ¹⁶ Verily, verily, I say unto you, The servant is not greater than his lord; neither he that is sent greater than he that sent him. ¹⁷ If ye know these things, happy are ye if ye do them.

10.1 The betrayal plot was known

Jesus would be betrayed by one of his own. However, that did not surprise him, because he knew about the plan to betray him (John 13:21).

Jesus' statement about his betrayal troubled the disciples, since they had just had supper. Peter asked Jesus to name the disciple who would betray him (John 13:24-25). Without hesitation, Jesus provided direct evidence of the disciple who will betray him (John 13:26-27).

After Judas took a break from Jesus, Satan entered him (John 13:27). Jesus was quick to inform Judas that whatever he had to do, he must do it quickly. As the Savior of the world, he knew he had come to die for the sins of people. His time was up, and he was not extending his stay on the earth. No effort was made by the Savior to prevent Judas from betraying him, since he was ready to die for all humanity.

John 13:18-30

¹⁸ I speak not of you all: I know whom I have chosen: but that the scripture may be fulfilled, He that eateth bread with me hath lifted up his heel against me. ¹⁹ Now I tell you before it come, that, when it is come to pass, ye may believe that I am

he. [20] Verily, verily, I say unto you, He that receiveth whomsoever I send receiveth me; and he that receiveth me receiveth him that sent me.

[21] When Jesus had thus said, he was troubled in spirit, and testified, and said, Verily, verily, I say unto you, that one of you shall betray me. [22] Then the disciples looked one on another, doubting of whom he spake. [23] Now there was leaning on Jesus' bosom one of his disciples, whom Jesus loved. [24] Simon Peter therefore beckoned to him, that he should ask who it should be of whom he spake. [25] He then lying on Jesus' breast saith unto him, Lord, who is it?

[26] Jesus answered, He it is, to whom I shall give a sop, when I have dipped it. And when he had dipped the sop, he gave it to Judas Iscariot, the son of Simon. [27] And after the sop Satan entered into him. Then said Jesus unto him, that thou doest, do quickly. [28] Now no man at the table knew for what intent he spake this unto him. [29] For some of them thought, because Judas had the bag, that Jesus had said unto him, Buy those things that we have need of against the feast; or, that he should give something to the poor. [30] He then having received the sop went immediately out: and it was night.

It was night time when Jesus had supper with his disciples and washed their feet. The disciples were probably expecting a joyful conversation with their Savior, but he only told them of the events leading up to his death. Their hearts were sorrowed, and to make things worse, Jesus informed them that one of his disciples would betray him.

10.2 Jesus walked to Gethsemane

After the Last Supper and the washing of the disciples' feet, Jesus walked to Gethsemane. On that occasion, only eleven disciples followed him, because Judas departed from Jesus after being overtaken by Satan.

Mark 14:32

[32] And they came to a place which was named Gethsemane: and he saith to his disciples, Sit ye here, while I shall pray.

10.3 Jesus prayed intensely at Gethsemane

As time drew near, Jesus went and prayed at Gethsemane. He took Peter, James, and John with him (Mark 14:33), and the three disciples fell asleep while Jesus went to pray. Persons often condemn the three disciples for sleeping; however, they must remember that these disciples had been working with the Master during the day. It was late night as they had supper, and Jesus had to take some time to both wash and dry their feet. Also, as they walked to Gethsemane, they ought to have been tired. When persons are inactive after a hard day's work, it becomes easy for them to sleep. The disciples' human bodies were already tired at midnight.

Mark 14:33-42

[33] And he taketh with him Peter and James and John, and began to be sore amazed, and to be very heavy; [34] And saith unto them, My soul is exceeding sorrowful unto death: tarry ye here, and watch. [35] And he went forward a little, and fell on the ground, and prayed that, if it were possible, the hour might pass from him. [36] And he said, Abba, Father, all things are possible unto thee; take away this cup from me: nevertheless not what I will, but what thou wilt.

[37] And he cometh, and findeth them sleeping, and saith unto Peter, Simon, sleepest thou? couldest not thou watch one hour? [38] Watch you and pray, lest ye enter into temptation. The spirit truly is ready, but the flesh is weak. [39] And again he went away, and prayed, and spake the same words. [40] And when he returned, he found them asleep again, (for their eyes were heavy,) neither wist they what to answer him. [41] And he cometh the third time, and saith unto them, Sleep on now, and take your rest: it is enough, the hour is come; behold, the Son of

man is betrayed into the hands of sinners. [42] Rise up, let us go; lo, he that betrayeth me is at hand.

Jesus prayed three times (Mark 14:32-41). On all three occasions, when he returned to the three disciples, they were asleep. He knew they were tired. However, it was important for him to pray. He prayed with great sorrow, as his time was at hand. He knew he must die and must also leave the disciples, whom he had developed great love for and friendship with.

10.4 The arrest of Jesus

After Judas left Jesus and the disciples, he went ahead and executed part of his plan. During the night, as Jesus was returning from the place where he went to pray, along with his eleven disciples, Judas and other religious leaders were waiting to arrest him (Mark 14:43-50).

Mark 14:43-52

[43] And immediately, while he yet spake, cometh Judas, one of the twelve, and with him a great multitude with swords and staves, from the chief priests and the scribes and the elders. [44] And he that betrayed him had given them a token, saying, Whomsoever I shall kiss, that same is he; take him, and lead him away safely. [45] And as soon as he was come, he goeth straightway to him, and saith, Master, master; and kissed him. [46] And they laid their hands on him, and took him.

[47] And one of them that stood by drew a sword, and smote a servant of the high priest, and cut off his ear. [48] And Jesus answered and said unto them, Are ye come out, as against a thief, with swords and with staves to take me? [49] I was daily with you in the temple teaching, and ye took me not: but the scriptures must be fulfilled. [50] And they all forsook him, and fled. [51] And there followed him a certain young man, having a linen cloth cast about his naked body; and the young men laid hold on him: [52] And he left the linen cloth, and fled from them naked.

Jesus did not resist his arrest. However, when they came to arrest him, he questioned them as to why they were using weapons to arrest him (Mark 14:48-49). They were aware that Jesus never carried weapons, since he was a man of peace: indeed, he is the Prince of Peace (Isaiah 9:6).

Judas used a friendly kiss to betray his former master. Following the kiss, it was time for Judas' team to arrest Jesus (Mark 14:44-46)

10.5 Jesus at the trial

After Jesus was arrested, then it was time to take him to trial. The trial of Jesus was conducted by many religious leaders. They looked for evidence to sentence Jesus, but they could not find any (Mark 14:56-60).

Mark 14:53-65

53 And they led Jesus away to the high priest: and with him were assembled all the chief priests and the elders and the scribes. 54 And Peter followed him afar off, even into the palace of the high priest: and he sat with the servants, and warmed himself at the fire. 55 And the chief priests and all the council sought for witness against Jesus to put him to death; and found none. 56 For much bare false witness against him, but their witness agreed not together. 57 And there arose certain, and bare false witness against him, saying, 58 We heard him say, I will destroy this temple that is made with hands, and within three days I will build another made without hands. 59 But neither so did their witness agree together.

60 And the high priest stood up in the midst, and asked Jesus, saying, Answerest thou nothing? what is it which these witness against thee? 61 But he held his peace, and answered nothing. Again the high priest asked him, and said unto him, Art thou the Christ, the Son of the Blessed?

62 And Jesus said, I am: and ye shall see the Son of man sitting on the right hand of power, and coming in the clouds of

heaven. [63] Then the high priest rent his clothes, and saith, What need we any further witnesses? [64] Ye have heard the blasphemy: what think ye? And they all condemned him to be guilty of death. [65] And some began to spit on him, and to cover his face, and to buffet him, and to say unto him, Prophesy: and the servants did strike him with the palms of their hands.

His accusers were ill prepared for the trial, using only second-hand statements (Mark 14:56-59). They trumped up a charge for blasphemy (Mark 14:64). They spat on him as he had predicted (Mark 14:65).

11. Jesus' crucifixion

The religious leaders were delighted that they were going to end Jesus' career. However, the crucifixion of Jesus was not the end of his ministry.

11.1 Jesus taken before Pilate and Herod

The religious leaders choose to punish Jesus by crucifixion. They felt it would be a great embarrassment to him and his followers.

Before he was put on the cross, he was beaten. Their actions caused much pain to his physical body.

Luke 23:1-25

¹ And the whole multitude of them arose, and led him unto Pilate. ² And they began to accuse him, saying, We found this fellow perverting the nation, and forbidding to give tribute to Caesar, saying that he himself is Christ a King. ³ And Pilate asked him, saying, Art thou the King of the Jews? And he answered him and said, Thou sayest it. ⁴ Then said Pilate to the chief priests and to the people, I find no fault in this man. ⁵ And they were the more fierce, saying, He stirreth up the people, teaching throughout all Jewry, beginning from Galilee to this place.

⁶ When Pilate heard of Galilee, he asked whether the man were a Galilean. ⁷ And as soon as he knew that he belonged unto Herod's jurisdiction, he sent him to Herod, who himself also was at Jerusalem at that time. ⁸ And when Herod saw Jesus, he was exceeding glad: for he was desirous to see him of a long season, because he had heard many things of him; and he hoped to have seen some miracle done by him. ⁹ Then he

questioned with him in many words; but he answered him nothing. ¹⁰And the chief priests and scribes stood and vehemently accused him. ¹¹And Herod with his men of war set him at nought, and mocked him, and arrayed him in a gorgeous robe, and sent him again to Pilate. ¹²And the same day Pilate and Herod were made friends together: for before they were at enmity between themselves.

¹³And Pilate, when he had called together the chief priests and the rulers and the people, ¹⁴Said unto them, Ye have brought this man unto me, as one that perverteth the people: and, behold, I, having examined him before you, have found no fault in this man touching those things whereof ye accuse him: ¹⁵No, nor yet Herod: for I sent you to him; and, lo, nothing worthy of death is done unto him. ¹⁶I will therefore chastise him, and release him. ¹⁷(For of necessity he must release one unto them at the feast.)

¹⁸And they cried out all at once, saying, Away with this man, and release unto us Barabbas: ¹⁹(Who for certain sedition made in the city, and for murder, was cast into prison.) ²⁰Pilate therefore, willing to release Jesus, spake again to them. ²¹But they cried, saying, Crucify him, crucify him. ²²And he said unto them the third time, Why, what evil hath he done? I have found no cause of death in him: I will therefore chastise him, and let him go. ²³And they were instant with loud voices, requiring that he might be crucified. And the voices of them and of the chief priests prevailed. ²⁴And Pilate gave sentence that it should be as they required. ²⁵And he released unto them him that for sedition and murder was cast into prison, whom they had desired; but he delivered Jesus to their will.

Figure 7. Accusations, punishments, and questioning of Jesus after his arrest (Luke 23)

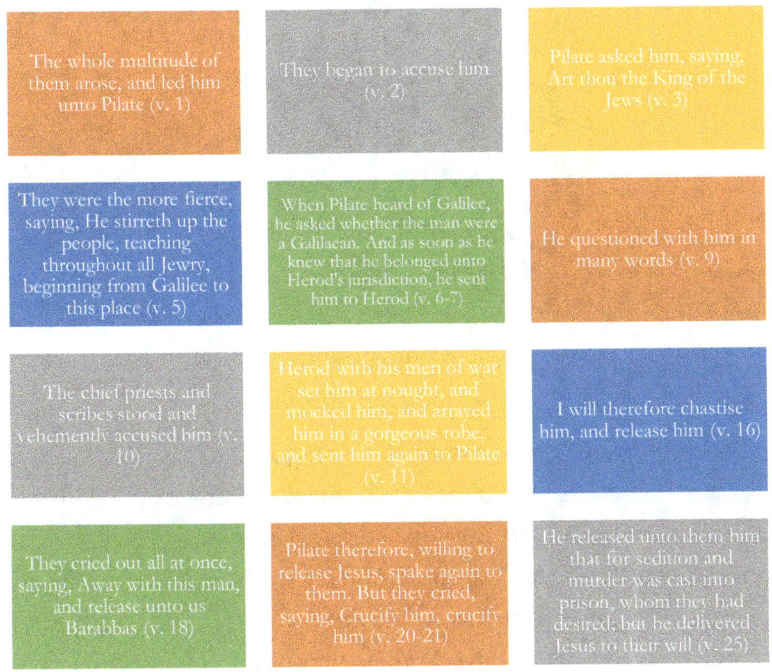

As much as the people tried to find legal reasons to arrest and punish Jesus for wrongdoing, they could not find justifiable legal reasons. Initially, the religious leaders took Jesus before Pilate to be tried (Luke 22:66-71, 23:1-7). After Pilate listened to them, he found no legal reasons to punish Jesus. During Jesus' trial, Pilate decided to send Jesus to Herod to be tried (Luke 23:6-7). After Herod listened to Jesus' accusers, he did not find any legal reasons to punish Jesus either (Luke 23:8-11), so he decided to send Jesus back to Pilate to be tried. After Pilate listened to the arguments of Jesus' accusers for the second time, he also found nothing new for which to punish Jesus (Luke 23:13-22).

Figure 8. Jesus was tried by Pilate and Herod

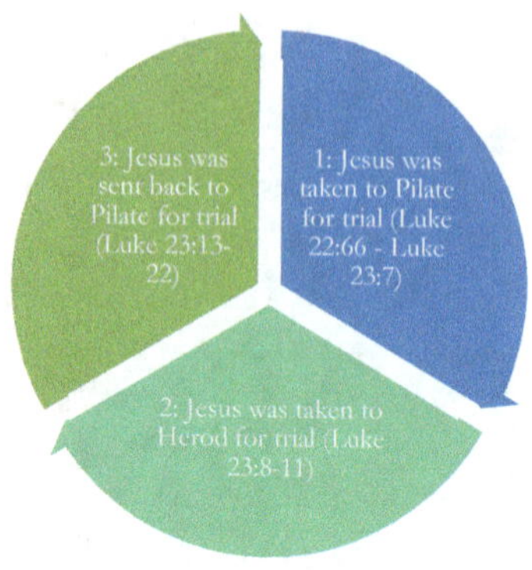

The second time around, Pilate still found no fault in Jesus. Pilate wanted to bring a peaceful end to these wrongful accusations. He gave Jesus' accusers two options: to choose either Jesus or Barabbas to be released. Many believers would expect that Jesus' accusers would have reconsidered their false accusation against him and let him go. However, they chose to free Barabbas and let Jesus be crucified. Their actions appeared cruel, but it was all part of God's plan for his Son to be crucified. If they had failed to do their part, then God's plan would not have been fulfilled.

Figure 9. Pilate's options for the accusers of Jesus, their choice, and their responses

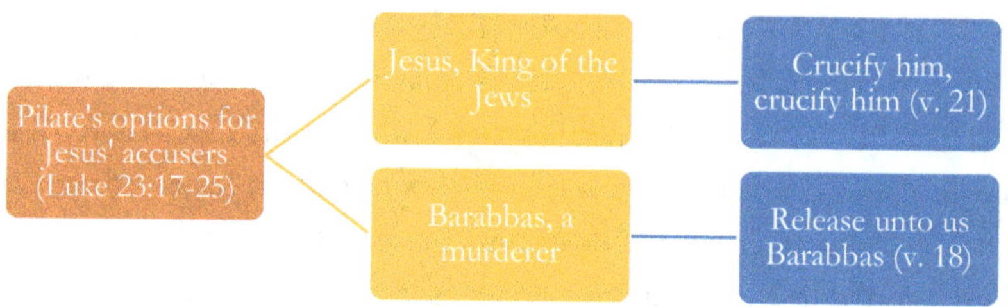

Pilate tried very hard to release Jesus, because there was no legal reason to punish him. However, Jesus' accusers were not going to allow Pilate to release him, as they had already made up their minds that Jesus must be punished.

The accusers of Jesus had two options to choose from. They decided that Barabbas should be released and Jesus should be crucified.

11.2 Jesus and the thieves to be crucified

After the religious leaders agreed that Jesus must be crucified, he had to walk to the place of crucifixion (Luke 23:26). There were some committed followers of Jesus who accompanied him (Luke 23:27-28).

Jesus was not the only person to be executed on that date. There were two criminals who were also there to be crucified (Luke 23:32). Before Jesus died, he asked his Father to forgive the people, for they did not know what they were doing (Luke 23:34).

Even as Jesus was about to die, people still accused him, and soldiers also mocked him (Luke 23:36-37). Over the head of Jesus was an inscription that indeed signified that he was King of the Jews (Luke 23:38). Even on the cross, Jesus had a conversation with one of the thieves. The thief asked Jesus to remember him, and Jesus give him his commitment (Luke 23:41-43).

Luke 23:26-43

26 And as they led him away, they laid hold upon one Simon, a Cyrenian, coming out of the country, and on him they laid the cross, that he might bear it after Jesus. 27 And there followed him a great company of people, and of women, which also bewailed and lamented him. 28 But Jesus turning unto them said, Daughters of Jerusalem, weep not for me, but weep for yourselves, and for your children. 29 For, behold, the days are coming, in the which they shall say, Blessed are the barren, and the wombs that never bare, and the paps which never gave suck. 30 Then shall they begin to say to the mountains, Fall on us; and to the hills, Cover us. 31 For if they do these things in a green tree, what shall be done in the dry?

32 And there were also two other, malefactors, led with him to be put to death. 33 And when they were come to the place, which is called Calvary, there they crucified him, and the

malefactors, one on the right hand, and the other on the left. [34] Then said Jesus, Father, forgive them; for they know not what they do. And they parted his raiment, and cast lots. [35] And the people stood beholding. And the rulers also with them derided him, saying, He saved others; let him save himself, if he be Christ, the chosen of God. [36] And the soldiers also mocked him, coming to him, and offering him vinegar, [37] And saying, If thou be the king of the Jews, save thyself.

[38] And a superscription also was written over him in letters of Greek, and Latin, and Hebrew, THIS IS THE KING OF THE JEWS. [39] And one of the malefactors which were hanged railed on him, saying, If thou be Christ, save thyself and us. [40] But the other answering rebuked him, saying, Dost not thou fear God, seeing thou art in the same condemnation? [41] And we indeed justly; for we receive the due reward of our deeds: but this man hath done nothing amiss. [42] And he said unto Jesus, Lord; remember me when thou comest into thy kingdom. [43] And Jesus said unto him, Verily I say unto thee, today shalt thou be with me in paradise.

11.3 Death of Jesus

From noon until 15:00 hours, there was darkness in the whole land (Luke 23:44-45). It was not a rainy day, but changes happened in the atmosphere. It had been a bright, sunny day, but the place now became dark. Jesus chose to give up his spirit unto the Father (Luke 23:46). This meant that Jesus was in full control of everything and was in communication with his Father. His earthly assignment was over.

Luke 23:44-49

[44] And it was about the sixth hour, and there was darkness over all the earth until the ninth hour. [45] And the sun was darkened, and the veil of the temple was rent in the midst. [46] And when Jesus had cried with a loud voice, he said, Father, into thy hands I commend my spirit: and having said thus, he gave up

the ghost. [47] Now when the centurion saw what was done, he glorified God, saying, Certainly this was a righteous man. [48] And all the people that came together to that sight, beholding the things which were done, smote their breasts, and returned. [49] And all his acquaintance, and the women that followed him from Galilee, stood afar off, beholding these things.

11.4 Jesus buried

Many persons looked on at what transpired with Jesus. While they might have wanted to help, Jesus had to go through the punishment to save humanity.

When it was confirmed that Jesus had died, then it was time to bury him. Joseph, a counsellor, asked for the body of Jesus in order to bury it properly (Luke 23:50). Joseph ensured that he obtained permission from Pilate to bury Jesus' body (Luke 23:51-53).

Luke 23:50-56

[50] And, behold, there was a man named Joseph, a counsellor; and he was a good man, and a just: [51] (The same had not consented to the counsel and deed of them;) he was of Arimathaea, a city of the Jews: who also himself waited for the kingdom of God. [52] This man went unto Pilate, and begged the body of Jesus. [53] And he took it down, and wrapped it in linen, and laid it in a sepulchre that was hewn in stone, wherein never man before was laid. [54] And that day was the preparation, and the sabbath drew on. [55] And the women also, which came with him from Galilee, followed after, and beheld the sepulchre, and how his body was laid. [56] And they returned, and prepared spices and ointments; and rested the sabbath day according to the commandment.

Some of the women who knew Jesus followed him to the place of crucifixion. They also followed Joseph to see where the body of Jesus was laid (Luke 23:55-56).

12. Up from the grave he arose

Those who crucified Jesus felt that they had defeated him. They were satisfied that he was dead. He was placed in the tomb, so this was expected to be the end of his life. Before he was placed in the tomb, his side was pierced and blood came out of body (John 19:34). They were convinced he was dead, so there was no need to break his legs (John 19:33).

John 19:31-37

[31] The Jews therefore, because it was the preparation, that the bodies should not remain upon the cross on the sabbath day, (for that sabbath day was an high day,) besought Pilate that their legs might be broken, and that they might be taken away. [32] Then came the soldiers, and brake the legs of the first, and of the other which was crucified with him. [33] But when they came to Jesus, and saw that he was dead already, they brake not his legs: [34] But one of the soldiers with a spear pierced his side, and forthwith came there out blood and water. [35] And he that saw it bare record, and his record is true: and he knoweth that he saith true, that ye might believe. [36] For these things were done, that the scripture should be fulfilled, A bone of him shall not be broken. [37] And again another scripture saith, They shall look on him whom they pierced.

12.1 Soldiers could not keep him in the tomb

The religious leaders sought permission to have soldiers guard the tomb. The soldiers changed shift regularly so that tired soldiers would never be protecting his tomb.

The Romans were anxious about Jesus' death and resurrection. If he was not a man of importance, why did they place so many guards to watch over his tomb (Matthew 27:62-66)? It is only when you are important that you will gain much attention. Not everyone celebrated Jesus' importance, but they knew that greatness was inside of the tomb.

Matthew 27:62-66

[62] Now the next day, that followed the day of the preparation, the chief priests and Pharisees came together unto Pilate, [63] Saying, Sir, we remember that that deceiver said, while he was yet alive, After three days I will rise again. [64] Command therefore that the sepulchre be made sure until the third day, lest his disciples come by night, and steal him away, and say unto the people, He is risen from the dead: so the last error shall be worse than the first. [65] Pilate said unto them, Ye have a watch: go your way, make it as sure as ye can. [66] So they went, and made the sepulchre sure, sealing the stone, and setting a watch.

12.2 He is a man of decency

Before Jesus came out of the tomb, he ensured that his clothes were in order. As a man of decency, he understood how to keep his temporary dwelling place tidy. When Peter and the other disciples looked into the tomb, they recognized that the clothes were well folded (John 20:5-7).

If anyone wants to follow Jesus, they must understand that he wants them to operate in a respectful manner. They must clean their external environment and he will cleanse their heart.

John 20:5-7

[5] And he stooping down, and looking in, saw the linen clothes lying; yet went he not in. [6] Then cometh Simon Peter following him, and went into the sepulchre, and seeth the linen clothes lie, [7] And the napkin, that was about his head, not lying with the linen clothes, but wrapped together in a place by itself.

12.3 The tomb is empty

Some of the women who were impacted by Jesus' ministry went to his tomb to visit his dead body. They went there with the intention of anointing his body with spices (Luke 24:1-2), as they wanted to give him a decent send-off. However, when they came close to the tomb, they saw that the stone had been rolled away. That was surprising to them, because they knew his dead body had been placed in the tomb and they did not expect anyone to steal it.

The women chose to look into the tomb, and they saw that his body was not there (Luke 24:3). In addition to the women confirming that Jesus' body was not in the tomb, Peter and some others also experienced the same thing (Luke 24:12).

Luke 24:1-12

[1] Now upon the first day of the week, very early in the morning, they came unto the sepulchre, bringing the spices which they had prepared, and certain others with them. [2] And they found the stone rolled away from the sepulchre. [3] And they entered in, and found not the body of the Lord Jesus.

[4] And it came to pass, as they were much perplexed thereabout, behold, two men stood by them in shining garments: [5] And as they were afraid, and bowed down their faces to the earth, they said unto them, Why seek ye the living among the dead? [6] He is not here, but is risen: remember how he spake unto you when he was yet in Galilee, [7] Saying, The Son of man must be delivered into the hands of sinful men, and be crucified, and the third day rise again.

[8] And they remembered his words, [9] And returned from the sepulchre, and told all these things unto the eleven, and to all the rest. [10] It was Mary Magdalene and Joanna, and Mary the mother of James, and other women that were with them, which told these things unto the apostles. [11] And their words seemed to them as idle tales, and they believed them not. [12] Then arose

Peter, and ran unto the sepulchre; and stooping down, he beheld the linen clothes laid by themselves, and departed, wondering in himself at that which was come to pass.

12.4 He visited many persons

The angel came from heaven and rolled back the stone so that the disciples could see that the tomb was empty (Matthew 28:2). Before Jesus ascended, he visited his disciples (Mark 16:9-14), which shows that he cares about people. He came to save people, and throughout his earthly journey, he always connected with people. He was a servant leader.

Jesus met with the women while they were returning from the grave (Matthew 28:9-10; Mark 16:9-14), which proved to them that he was no longer in the grave. Jesus gave the disciples and the women first-hand experience that he had risen. If he had not proven to them that he was alive, many persons would still have believed the lies of the Roman soldiers that his body was stolen by his followers.

12.5 Jesus walked and talked with two persons on the Emmaus road

Some persons were concerned about Jesus' death. While two persons were speaking about Jesus' death (Luke 24:13), he joined them and had a conversation with them. They invited him to their house and he went with them (Luke 24:28-29). Jesus made himself known to them as he took bread, blessed it, gave thanks, and then gave it to them. They recognized him by his actions. After they saw what he did, they fled, because they realized that they were walking and talking with Jesus and had not recognized that it was him (Luke 24:30-31).

Luke 24:13-35

[13] And, behold, two of them went that same day to a village called Emmaus, which was from Jerusalem about threescore furlongs. [14] And they talked together of all these things which had happened. [15] And it came to pass, that, while they communed together and reasoned, Jesus himself drew near,

and went with them. ¹⁶But their eyes were holden that they should not know him.

¹⁷ And he said unto them, What manner of communications are these that ye have one to another, as ye walk, and are sad? ¹⁸ And the one of them, whose name was Cleopas, answering said unto him, Art thou only a stranger in Jerusalem, and hast not known the things which are come to pass there in these days? ¹⁹ And he said unto them, What things? And they said unto him, Concerning Jesus of Nazareth, which was a prophet mighty in deed and word before God and all the people: ²⁰ And how the chief priests and our rulers delivered him to be condemned to death, and have crucified him. ²¹ But we trusted that it had been he which should have redeemed Israel: and beside all this, today is the third day since these things were done. ²² Yea, and certain women also of our company made us astonished, which were early at the sepulchre; ²³ And when they found not his body, they came, saying, that they had also seen a vision of angels, which said that he was alive. ²⁴ And certain of them which were with us went to the sepulchre, and found it even so as the women had said: but him they saw not.

²⁵ Then he said unto them, O fools, and slow of heart to believe all that the prophets have spoken: ²⁶ Ought not Christ to have suffered these things, and to enter into his glory? ²⁷ And beginning at Moses and all the prophets, he expounded unto them in all the scriptures the things concerning himself. ²⁸ And they drew nigh unto the village, whither they went: and he made as though he would have gone further. ²⁹ But they constrained him, saying, Abide with us: for it is toward evening, and the day is far spent. And he went in to tarry with them.

³⁰ And it came to pass, as he sat at meat with them, he took bread, and blessed it, and brake, and gave to them. ³¹ And their eyes were opened, and they knew him; and he vanished out of their sight. ³² And they said one to another, Did not our heart

burn within us, while he talked with us by the way, and while he opened to us the scriptures? ³³ And they rose up the same hour, and returned to Jerusalem, and found the eleven gathered together, and them that were with them, ³⁴ Saying, The Lord is risen indeed, and hath appeared to Simon. ³⁵ And they told what things were done in the way, and how he was known of them in breaking of bread.

12.6 Jesus met with the eleven disciples

After Jesus was risen, he moved around to many persons. He continued to work with the disciples and chose to visit them so that they would know he had arisen from the grave after the third day. He had already informed people that he would destroy the temple in three days and build it again. He was not referring to a physical temple, but to his own body.

When he visited the disciples, they were afraid (Luke 24:36) and thought he was a ghost (Luke 24:37). Because of their doubts, Jesus provided evidence to them that he was the same Jesus who was crucified (Luke 24:38-41). Jesus had fellowship with the disciples and ate among them to prove that he was the same Jesus (Luke 24:41-43).

Luke 24:38-49

³⁸ And he said unto them, Why are ye troubled? and why do thoughts arise in your hearts? ³⁹ Behold my hands and my feet, that it is I myself: handle me, and see; for a spirit hath not flesh and bones, as ye see me have. ⁴⁰ And when he had thus spoken, he shewed them his hands and his feet. ⁴¹ And while they yet believed not for joy, and wondered, he said unto them, Have ye here any meat? ⁴² And they gave him a piece of a broiled fish, and of an honeycomb. ⁴³ And he took it, and did eat before them.

⁴⁴ And he said unto them, These are the words which I spake unto you, while I was yet with you, that all things must be fulfilled, which were written in the law of Moses, and in the

prophets, and in the psalms, concerning me. ⁴⁵ Then opened he their understanding, that they might understand the scriptures, ⁴⁶ And said unto them, Thus it is written, and thus it behooved Christ to suffer, and to rise from the dead the third day: ⁴⁷ And that repentance and remission of sins should be preached in his name among all nations, beginning at Jerusalem. ⁴⁸ And ye are witnesses of these things. ⁴⁹ And, behold, I send the promise of my Father upon you: but tarry ye in the city of Jerusalem, until ye be endued with power from on high.

12.7 Jesus departs from the earth

Jesus reminded the disciples of many of the things he had spoken to them about. Before he ascended, he blessed them (Luke 24:50).

Luke 24:50-53

⁵⁰ And he led them out as far as to Bethany, and he lifted up his hands, and blessed them. ⁵¹ And it came to pass, while he blessed them, he was parted from them, and carried up into heaven. ⁵² And they worshipped him, and returned to Jerusalem with great joy: ⁵³ And were continually in the temple, praising and blessing God. Amen.

Jesus was sent by the Father to be on the earth. After his earthly assignment was over, he went back to heaven (Luke 24:51). He will be coming again to rapture those who believe in him.

12.8 He wants to live in every believer

Jesus no longer lives in the grave. If persons visit the grave, as the disciples did, they will recognize that it is empty. The question is, where can anyone find Jesus today? He is in neither the pharmacy nor the supermarket. He can be neither bought nor sold. However, his death gave life to every believer. When they put him to death, they gave him the opportunity to live in the heart of every believer. If you do not have him in your heart today, then it is important that you invite him to be Lord in your life.

Jesus promised to send the Comforter (John 16:13-16). Today, through the Holy Spirit, believers have a better understanding of Jesus, who now lives in them. When Jesus ascended, the Holy Spirit descended on those who waited for him (Acts 1:8-11).

12.9 Believers must continue to do the works of Jesus

Since Jesus has risen and the Spirit of God is in believers, they can go ahead and fulfill the Great Commission (Matthew 28:18-20). Believers must continue the works of Jesus on this earth, since he has given us the power to represent him on this earth.

Believers must know that they are not powerless, but powerful. Those who believe in Jesus will receive his power.

John 1:12

[12] But as many as received him, to them gave the power to become the sons of God, even to them that believe on his name.

The gospel must be preached to all corners of the earth. While many believers are comfortable within the sanctuaries that they fellowship in, they must use every opportunity to share the gospel with others.

Matthew 28:18-20

[18] And Jesus came and spake unto them, saying, All power is given unto me in heaven and in earth. [19] Go you therefore, and teach all nations, baptizing them in the name of the Father, and of the Son, and of the Holy Ghost: [20] teaching them to observe all things whatsoever I have commanded you: and, lo, I am with you always, even unto the end of the world. Amen.

Figure 10. Go and help others when you are saved

Stage 1 (Sinner)	Stage 2 (Salvation)	Stage 3 (Seeking souls for God's kingdom)
You are a sinner and need salvation (Romans 3:23)	Christ has saved you and empowered you (1 John 1:6-9)	As you are empowered, share the gospel with all people (Matthew 28:18-20)

Judas' betrayal was all part of God's plan. Jesus was betrayed by religious people, but he came for sinners and not the righteous. When Jesus was placed in the tomb, people thought it was the end of his ministry, but today, he is alive forevermore and now sits at the right hand of God, making intercession for the saints.

Hebrews 12:1-3

[1] Wherefore seeing we also are compassed about with so great a cloud of witnesses, let us lay aside every weight, and the sin which doth so easily beset us, and let us run with patience the race that is set before us, [2] Looking unto Jesus the author and finisher of our faith; who for the joy that was set before him endured the cross, despising the shame, and is set down at the right hand of the throne of God. [3] For consider him that endured such contradiction of sinners against himself, lest ye be wearied and faint in your minds.

About the author

Jesus Christ remains the focus of all believers' salvation and faith. His birth is as significant as his death, and so Rev. Geary Reid saw the need to encapsulate Jesus' birth, death, and resurrection in one literature.

On 17 April 2022, Rev. Geary Reid had to preach two services about the resurrection of Jesus Christ, since it was Resurrection Sunday. He searched among the collection of books he has authored and recognized that none of them addressed this important topic. Therefore, he decided to put his thoughts into writing, and hence this literature was produced. He knows that if believers want to celebrate Christmas and Easter, they ought to have one literature that covers much of the information they need to know about these two important annual Christian celebrations.

Rev. Reid knows that the birth of Jesus was not an unplanned event. As he searched the scriptures, he found that there is much evidence that God planned the birth and death of Jesus. After Adam and Eve sinned, God immediately implemented his redemptive plan, since God wants to save his people from their sins.

All believers must be knowledgeable about who Jesus is, why he came to the earth, and the fact that he existed before the earth was formed. Since believers are God's representatives on the earth, they must know the truth about this man called "Jesus." Geary Reid is not ashamed of his Savior. In 1986 he gave his life to the Lord, and in March 1989 he went down into the water to be baptized. He continues to spend considerable time getting to know more about his Lord, and also presenting the Savior to others.

There are many persons who do not know the Savior. They must equip themselves with the Word of God and then share the gospel with those who are still sinners. Geary Reid wants to remind believers to let it remain their burden to share Jesus wherever they go. Not everyone will be assigned senior leadership within their churches, but everyone still has the responsibility to encourage others to accept the Savior.

The crucifixion of Jesus was cruel, but he died for sinners like Geary Reid. Today, Rev. Reid is excited to introduce the one who saved him from his sins and from going to a lost eternity.

www.ingramcontent.com/pod-product-compliance
Lightning Source LLC
Chambersburg PA
CBHW070547160726
48003CB00005B/1924